LEADE

FATHOM BIBLE STUDIES

the passion
THE DEATH AND RESURRECTION OF JESUS

FATH◯M

A DEEP DIVE INTO THE STORY OF GOD

FATHOM: THE PASSION
THE DEATH AND RESURRECTION OF JESUS
LEADER GUIDE

Scripture quotations unless noted otherwise are from the Common English Bible. Copyright © 2011 by the Common English Bible. All rights reserved. Used by permission. *www.CommonEnglishBible.com.*

Writer: Katie Heierman
Editor: Ben Howard
Designer: Keely Moore

Websites are constantly changing. Although the websites recommended in this resource were checked at the time this unit was developed, we recommend that you double-check all sites to verify that they are still live and that they are still suitable for students before doing the activity.

ISBN: 9781501838637

PACP10508962-01

17 18 19 20 21 22 23 24 25 26 — 10 9 8 7 6 5 4 3 2 1

MANUFACTURED IN THE UNITED STATES OF AMERICA

CONTENTS

About Fathom

Fathom.

It's such a big word. It feels endless and deep. It's the kind of word that feels like it should only be uttered by James Earl Jones with the bass turned all the way up.

Which means it's the perfect word to talk about a God who's infinite and awe-inspiring. It's also the perfect word for a book like the Bible that's filled with miracles and inspiration, but also wrestles with stories of violence and pain and loss.

The mission of *Fathom* is to dive deep into the story of God that we find in the Bible. You'll encounter Scriptures filled with inspiration and encouragement, and you'll also explore passages that are more complicated and challenging.

Each lesson will focus on one passage, but will also launch into the larger context of how God's story is being told through that passage. More importantly, each lesson will explore how God's story is intimately tied to our own stories, and how a God who is beyond our imagination can also be a God who loves us deeply and personally.

We invite you to wrestle with this and more as we dive deep into God's story.

How to Use This Book

First, we want to thank you for teaching this class! While we strive to provide the best material possible for leaders and students, we know that your personal connection with your teens is the most important part of the lesson.

With that out of the way, welcome to the *Fathom Leader Guide*. Each lesson is designed around Kolb's Learning Cycle and moves students through five sections: *Sync, Tour, Reveal, Build,* and *After.*

Sync introduces the students to the general theme of each lesson with a fun activity. There is both a high-energy and low-energy option to choose from in each lesson. *Tour* is the meat of the lesson and focuses intensely on the central Scripture each week. *Reveal* is a time for reflection where youth can digest the information they've heard and start to make to process it. Then the *Build* section puts this newfound knowledge to practice using creative activities and projects. Finally, *After* gives the students options for practices to try throughout the week to reinforce the central concept of the lesson.

Additionally, before each lesson, a Theology and Commentary section is provided to give you a little more information about the topic being discussed that week.

This Leader Guide is designed to be used hand-in-hand with the *Fathom Student Journal*. Each student will need a journal, and the journals should be kept in the class at the end of the lesson. At the end of the study, give the students their journals as a keepsake to remember what they've learned.

Finally, at the end of this book we've included an Explore More section that offers short outlines for additional lessons if you and your class want to keep diving into these Scriptures after the end of this four-week study.

The Fathom 66 Bible Genre Guid

ENTER ZIP OR LOCATION [ ]

Stories ♡ [TICKETS]

★★★★☆

Showtimes: Parts of Genesis, Joshua, Judges, Ruth, 1 Samuel, 2 Samuel, 1 Kings, 2 Kings, 1 Chronicles, 2 Chronicles, Ezra, Nehemiah, Esther, Matthew, Mark, Luke, John, Acts

The Law ♡ [TICKETS]

★★★★★

Showtimes: Parts of Genesis, Exodus, Leviticus, Numbers, Deuteronomy

Wisdom ♡ [TICKETS]

★★★★★

Showtimes: Job, Some Psalms, Proverbs, Ecclesiastes, Song of Solomon, Lamentations, James

Psalms ♡ [TICKETS]

★★★★★

Showtimes: Psalms

The Prophets ♡ [TICKETS]

★★★★★

Showtimes: Isaiah, Jeremiah, Ezekiel, Hosea, Joel, Amos, Obadiah, Jonah, Michah, Nahum, Habakkuk, Zephaniah, Haggai, Zechariah, Malachi

Letters ♡ [TICKETS]

★★★★★

Showtimes: Romans, 1 Corinthians, 2 Corinthians, Galatians, Ephesians, Philippians, Colossians, 1 Thessalonians, 2 Thessalonians, 1 Timothy, 2 Timothy, Titus, Philemon, Hebrews, James, 1 Peter, 2 Peter, 1 John, 2 John, 3 John, Jude

Apocalyptic Writings ♡ [TICKETS]

★★★★★

Showtimes: Daniel, Revelation

The Fathom Bible Storylines

Create (1)

Invite (I)

Act (A)

Redeem (R)

Experience (E)

Hope (H)

Introduction to The Passion

Background

We've all had one of those weeks—a week where our life is turned completely upside down from what it was when the week arrived. It may look like losing a job, the end of a relationship, or the death of a loved one.

When we study the Passion of Jesus, we are invited to journey with Jesus through one of those weeks. These Scriptures teach us important things about Jesus, and ultimately show us the true heart of God.

God hurts when we hurt. God cries when we cry. God rejoices when we are overcome with joy. Through Jesus' example, we see all of this and so much more.

As you embark on this study, I pray that you come to it with an attitude of expectation. Don't receive the story of Holy Week the same way you've always done it before. Instead, expect that God will reveal God's infinite love and grace to you in a fresh way. Dive into these Scriptures knowing that you will emerge with something new.

Over our time together, we'll explore Jesus' entry into Jerusalem, his visit to the temple, and an odd interaction with a fig tree. We'll hear the story of the woman who anointed Jesus with oil and Jesus' own example of humility when he washed the feet of his followers. These are stories you've likely heard before, but think about what you might discover as you start to consider them as part of a single story and open your eyes to the nature of God in Jesus.

We'll also explore the pain that Jesus felt—the abandonment, betrayal, and loneliness that led up to his crucifixion. We'll see Jesus at his most vulnerable, crying out to God, and we'll be reminded that in this vulnerability, Jesus gives us an example of how we, too, can be open to God about our pain and sorrow.

I invite you to allow God to work in you during the next four weeks. Remember that Jesus, both fully God and fully human, walked through this life in the same way that you do. As we walk through this week with him, keep your eyes open for the ways Jesus shows us how God continues to be with his created people.

Fathom Strategy for Reading and Understanding the Bible

"The Bible is written for us, but not to us."

This where we start on our quest. When we read the Bible, we have to constantly remember that the Bible is written for us, but not to us. Understanding the original context of the Bible helps us ask the right questions when interpreting Scripture.

For the first steps in our process, we need to understand how each passage we read functions in context and examine the historical background. When we read a passage, we should ask questions about the era, location, and culture of the original audience, as well as how a particular writing relates to the larger narrative of the Bible. This strategy not only helps us understand a passage's primary meaning, it also gives us guidance on how to translate that meaning into our specific circumstances today.

FATH●M
Deep Cleaning

Summary

Students will study and reflect on Jesus' arrival into Jerusalem and explore the ways that Jesus' arrival disrupted normal religious practices of the time.

Overview

- **Sync** students with the idea that thinking and acting differently can make things uncomfortable for others.
- **Tour** through the Gospel Scriptures covering the entry to Jerusalem, Jesus cleansing the temple, and the cursing of the fig tree.
- **Reveal** how the Scripture connects to students and how they can create change in the midst of opposition.
- **Build** a new understanding of the story of Jesus' entry into Jerusalem by having the students create a comic strip depicting the Gospel narrative.
- **After** the lesson, challenge the students to share what they've learned with others by putting these lessons into practice.

Anchor Point

- Matthew 21:10-11—*And when Jesus entered Jerusalem, the whole city was stirred up. "Who is this?" they asked. The crowds answered, "It's the prophet Jesus from Nazareth in Galilee."*

Supplies

- Student Journals
- Pens or pencils
- Disposable cups
- Posterboard
- Markers
- Colored pencils
- Sheets of drawing paper
- Quiet background music (optional)

Parent E-mail

We are starting a new series this week about the story of Jesus' arrest and crucifixion, as well as some of the stories leading up to the Passion narrative. To help drive home the points your students are learning, we recommend that you ask your students about the lesson each week. Here are some other ways to engage this week:

- Ask your student about places where she or he feels called to stand up for what is right.
- As a family, read through the story of Jesus from the Last Supper through the Resurrection. Talk about what you feel when you read this story.

Leader Notes

The Gospel accounts of Jesus' arrest and crucifixion show us strength, wisdom, and courage. But most importantly, Jesus teaches us that we can't make him into whatever we want. The Pharisees couldn't make him behave. The people couldn't make him rule over them or overtake the political leaders. And we can't make Jesus fit into our own boxes.

Encourage your students to be constantly aware of what Jesus said he was as opposed to what people wanted him to be. Isn't God's way always better, even when we can't understand in the moment?

Theology and Commentary

Jesus made his entry into Jerusalem during the Jewish season of Passover. Specifically, he arrived on "Nisan Day 10," which is the day when each home would choose a young, unblemished lamb to present for sacrifice. Many theologians draw the connection that Jesus made his entry into the city knowing he would be sacrificed, just like the lambs would on that same day.

On a day when attention was normally focused on the traditions of Passover, instead the crowds were shouting, "Hosanna!" to the man who appeared to go against the sentiments of religious leaders like the Pharisees, a man who regularly challenged their understanding of the law. As you read through this section, take note of how uncomfortable and disapproving the Pharisees are over Jesus' actions and his direct challenges to the status quo.

Another key to understanding today's lesson is exploring the different perspectives of the Gospels. It is important to remind students that these varying perspectives grant us a broader understanding of the story of Jesus and especially the Passion narrative.

1. Matthew

The Book of Matthew was written to Jewish Christians who were already aware of Jesus but still valued the Law of Moses. These two things contradict each other as much as they complement each other. The writer of Matthew uses the teachings of Jesus to show Jewish Christians a new way to think about their faith. Faith is about more than rules and laws; faith changes the way we live our lives.

To further connect with the Jewish Christian community, Matthew highlights moments when Jesus is fulfilling the law and the prophets from the Old Testament. It also highlights the differences between Jesus and the religious leaders of the day, and how Jesus' understanding of Scripture went deeper than that of many of those with whom he butted heads. With this in mind, ask the students to read Matthew from the perspective of someone who deeply values the traditions of the Old Testament and the perspective of religious leaders.

2. Mark

The Book of Mark is the shortest of the Gospels. As we read through it, we get a no-nonsense vibe from the way it is written. This book introduces us to a more radical side of Jesus than Matthew does. You can almost call Mark the action-movie version of the Gospels.

Mark is clearly written to a Gentile audience that has little familiarity with Jewish tradition. This is made clear by the way Mark takes time to explain Jewish traditions to its audience. Encourage your youth to note these explanations of Jewish tradition in Mark.

Mark also includes a number of little extras that we only read about in Mark. For example, in the account of the arrest in Gethsemane in Mark 14, we are told of a young disciple who runs off naked after the guards pull off his clothes as they try to grab him. Some theorize that this young disciple was Mark himself, and this was his way of writing himself into history.

3. Luke

Luke is the Gospel with the strongest storytelling. Most people can probably recite parts of Luke 2 (the Nativity story), even if they've never been to church. When I was in high school, my pastor used to talk about life being in the journey, not the destination. That's the feel we get with Luke. It's not so much where they go as what happens on the way there.

It is written to an educated Greek audience that is likely already Christian. You can tell this from the inscription to *Theophilus*, a name that literally means "love of God." Luke is largely an accumulation of firsthand accounts that the author has put together to tell the story of Jesus. Luke's journalistic account provides a particular perspective that reminds us to keep our eyes open for the details around us. Encourage youth to pay attention to the details as they read the Book of Luke.

4. John

The other three Gospels are often called the Synoptic Gospels because they contain many of the same stories. The Gospel of John is way different. While the other Gospels are mainly interested in telling the story of Jesus while occasionally mentioning his divine nature, John is focused on explaining that Jesus was both God and man.

Most of Jesus' "I Am" statements are found in John, which helps to ground the Gospel in the Old Testament accounts of God, who says God's name is "I Am." John also refers to himself throughout the book as "the disciple whom Jesus loved," which pulls us into a new understanding of Jesus as one who personally loves each of his disciples. Encourage your students to read the Book of John from the perspective of "the disciple whom Jesus loved" as they look for all the ways that John points out Jesus' divinity.

Leader Reflection

When I was a little kid, my cousin—who lived four hours away—and I decided we were going to become pen pals. For Christmas that year, we both received these cool invisible ink pens. Each pen had a special light that allowed you to read what it said. We thought we were so special because we could see what our parents couldn't since they didn't have super-cool pens like us.

The Gospel narratives in this lesson begin with the triumphal entry and then move on to Jesus overturning the tables in the temple and cursing a fig tree. Throughout the text are scattered tidbits about the disapproval and anger the Pharisees felt in light of Jesus' actions. This disapproval provides a perfect opportunity to ask students to share where they feel disapproval even if they don't yet understand why.

This conversation is important because, despite the intensity of the other aspects of the Passion story, students seem to struggle understanding this section the most. Why are the Pharisees so mad? Why do the people ultimately turn on Jesus? Why does Jesus get so angry in the temple and with the fig tree? There is a lot to be decoded. It reminds me of my invisible pen. The recipient can only understand the message if he or she has the special pen with the special light.

You are that light for your students. Encourage them to speak up and ask questions when there are gaps in their understanding. Even if you don't know the answer, you can still have an amazing discussion with your group. You're going to be great! We're praying for you, and we encourage you to pray for yourself and your students this week as well.

NOTES

SYNC (5-10 minutes)

High-Energy Option—Flipping Out

[Pass out two disposable cups to each youth. You can use any size cups that you have easy access to.]

SAY: We're going to split into two teams, Team A and Team B.

[Split class into two teams.]

SAY: Team A is going to take their cups and scatter them around the room facing up. Team B is going to scatter their cups around the room facing down.

[Give both teams a few moments to place their cups.]

SAY: When I say "Go," Team A will try to turn all the cups right side up. Team B will try to turn all the cups so that they face down. When I say "Stop," the team with the most cups facing their direction wins.

[Play the game for a few minutes.]

ASK: What was the most frustrating part of this game?

[Let a few students respond.]

ASK: Have you ever been in a situation where you were trying to do one thing, but it felt like others were doing the complete opposite?

[When the students respond, ask them how it felt when they were in this situation.]

SAY: This week we're going to be discussing the ways that Jesus flipped over the way the Pharisees had always done things, both literally and metaphorically.

Low-Energy Option—Honey, Do You Love Me?

SAY: First, all of you need to take your chairs and circle up. Next, I'm going to need a volunteer, and I need that volunteer to be someone who is comfortable embarrassing themselves.

[Select a student as a volunteer.]

SAY (to the volunteer): Okay, your task is to go to someone in this circle and ask, "Honey, do you love me?" Your goal is to make the person smile.

SAY (to the class): The person chosen has a simple task. You have to keep a straight face and say, "Honey, I love you, but I just can't smile." If you can respond without smiling, then our lovelorn volunteer has to continue on to another person. If you do crack, then you have to take the volunteer's place.

[Play a few rounds of the game, no more than a few minutes.]

ASK: Those of you who cracked, what made you smile?

[Wait for a few answers.]

ASK: Did anyone get a little nervous or feel awkward?

[When students respond, ask them why they felt that way.]

SAY: In our lesson today, we're going to discuss some socially awkward things that Jesus did that made other people uncomfortable and talk about why he chose to act that way.

TOUR (10-15 minutes)

ASK: What do you think of when you hear the word *passion*?

[Affirm every response. If someone mentions the story of Jesus' crucifixion, then skip the next question.]

ASK: Have any of you ever heard the word *passion* used to talk about Jesus or the story of his crucifixion? What have you heard?

[Take a few responses from students.]

SAY: Chances are that you've heard the story of the Passion so many times before that you could easily tell it. It's the story of Holy Week, of Jesus' arrival in Jerusalem, and his arrest, trial, crucifixion, and resurrection.

In this context, *passion* relates to suffering. It's taken from the Greek word *pascho* which means "to suffer." As we continue through this study, think about the ways Jesus suffered and what that suffering means.

To take a look at the beginning of this story, I'm going to need you to split up into four groups.

[Assign each group one of the following passages: Matthew 21:1-22; Mark 11:1-19; Luke 19:29-48; and John 12:12-19. If you have a smaller class, you can read through these verses collectively or assign one passage to each student.]

SAY: With your group, read through the passage you've been assigned multiple times. Afterward, write down on the posterboard provided to you the key things that happen in the passage so that you can share with the rest of the class.

[Distribute posterboard and markers to each group. Make sure that your groups hit the following points in their respective passages. Offer them hints if they are struggling.]

Matthew—disciples getting the donkey, entry into the city, pushing over tables in the temple, healing those in need, cursing the fig tree.

Mark—disciples finding the colt, Jesus riding the colt, crowd cheering, cursing the fig tree, Jesus in the temple, chief priests plotting.

Luke—disciples retrieving colt, praising God because of Jesus, "if they were silent, the stones would shout," Jesus weeping, destruction-of-temple prophecy, throwing out merchants in the temple, plotting to kill Jesus.

John—Jesus riding in on the young donkey, crowd cheering and waving, confused disciples, frustrated Pharisees.

SAY: Let's have everybody gather together again. Who wants to share what they found in their assigned verses first?

[You might want to add in some of the key details mentioned above if the group forgets to mention them.]

ASK: What are some similarities you noticed among the passages? What are some differences?

[When anyone mentions a difference, ask why they think the accounts are different. (Answer: They were written by different authors who had different sources and were emphasizing different parts of the story for the audiences they were writing to.)]

ASK: Did anyone notice places where Jesus did something odd or where he did something that would upset the Pharisees? Why do you think he did that?

REVEAL (10 minutes)

SAY: For the next few minutes, spend some time thinking and writing about the questions in your Student Journal. You don't need to answer all of them. Try to focus on the ones that most intrigue you. In a few minutes, I will call you back together and we'll share some of your responses.

[If your group has a hard time with silence, you can play some quiet music in the background. After seven or eight minutes, call the group back together and ask for volunteers who want to share their responses.]

Journal Questions

1. Does the "grand entrance" look like what you'd imagine a grand entrance to look like?
2. Were you surprised to read how Jesus cleared out the temple? Why?
3. Why do you think Jesus got mad at and cursed a fig tree? What could the fig tree have symbolized?
4. What things would you like to see happen in your church or community that you feel are resisted by adults or church leaders? What are some ways you could try to convince them about why your ideas are important?

BUILD (15-20 minutes)

SAY: I need everybody to get together in groups of three.

[Allow groups to gather together. Pass out paper, markers, and colored pencils as they get together.]

SAY: It's time to get creative! If you turn to the Build section in your Student Journal, you'll see the familiar frames of a comic. With your group, use this framework to sketch out a comic of the narrative we learned about today.

[Give the students three or four minutes to sketch out the ideas for their comic.]

SAY: Now that you've sketched out the framework, use the paper and art supplies available to work together and draw a large-scale version of the comic you've sketched out.

[Give the students ten to fifteen minutes to draw the comic on the paper provided and then post it on the wall of the room to show the entire story.]

ASK: Were there parts of the story that leapt out to you more when you drew them?

[When the students respond, ask them why they were drawn to these parts of the story.]

ASK: Does seeing the story in another medium help you understand it better? What insights did you gain by drawing this story?

AFTER (5 minutes)

SAY: This week I want you to reflect on what you wrote in the Reveal section today. Take a picture of it on your phone and in a few days, I'll text you and remind you to revisit it.

[After they've taken pictures of the Reveal section in their Student Journals, invite the students to participate in an After activity. Remind them about it during the week.]

The Change You Want to See

SAY: This week find a video or image that conveys the kind of change you want to see happen in the world. Make sure it's something real and that it's something positive. Then share it with all your friends and followers on social media.

Family Surprise

SAY: Sometime this week, do something to surprise your parents, siblings, or other family members in a good way. For example, wash the dishes or take out the trash without being asked. Try to give as many positive surprises as you can this week to create positive change in your home.

PRAYER

SAY: Let's close in prayer together.

LEADER: God, open our eyes.

YOUTH: Let us see your passion.

LEADER: God, mold our hearts.

YOUTH: Let us become who you've called us to be.

LEADER: God, give us strength.

YOUTH: Let us stand firm in the face of opposition.

LEADER: We love you.

YOUTH: We love you.

ALL: Amen.

FATH●M
Presence

Summary

This lesson highlights the importance of love in community. This love is particularly evident in Jesus' interactions with his disciples during the Last Supper and the events leading up to it.

Overview

- **Sync** students with the importance of presence by challenging them to recognize how they rely on others.
- **Tour** through the events leading up to and including the Last Supper through a series of experiential readings.
- **Reveal** another side of the familiar stories of the anointing of Jesus and the Last Supper by asking students to re-envision them in new contexts.
- **Build** on these revelations by empowering students to use their creative abilities to tell the story of Jesus and his followers.
- **After** the lesson, challenge the students to try one of the activities and be present with others this week.

Anchor Point

- John 13:19-20—*I'm telling you this now, before it happens, so that when it does happen you will believe that I Am. I assure you that whoever receives someone I send receives me, and whoever receives me receives the one who sent me.*

Supplies

- Student Journals
- Pens or pencils
- Blindfold
- Two or three difficult-to-describe objects
- Flip chart
- Markers
- Essential oil and diffuser
- Towel, washcloth, bowl of water
- Loaf of bread and cup of grape juice
- Internet access and large-screen device
- Paint and brushes
- Blank paper

Parent E-mail

This week we are continuing our study on the Passion by looking at the Last Supper and the events that led up to it. Through this lesson, youth will learn about the importance of being present in community. To help bring this point home, here are some ways to engage this week:

- Plan one night this week to have a special family dinner. Sit down at the table, put away electronics, and spend time with one another.
- Tell funny stories from when you were a teenager or talk about your favorite family memories. The main thing is to take time to connect with your family.

Leader Notes

Teenagers live with a lot of fear. From fears about school and friendships to fears about family and relationships to fears about natural disasters or the future, there are so many complicated, overwhelming things facing teens.

As you teach your group about the precious presence of Jesus, remember that you offer them more than games and pizza. You are offering them a chance to come face-to-face with a God who will be there through all their trials and who can soothe their fears. They encounter God when we listen and share with them, when we are present with them. The best way you can love your students is simply to be with them.

Theology and Commentary

This week before the lesson, be sure to read Matthew 26:6-13; John 13:1-20; Mark 14:10-26; and 1 Corinthians 11:23-26.

As you guide your students through these passages, here is some key information that might help you in fully sharing the story.

The Anointing: Matthew 26:6-13

In John Wesley's commentary on Matthew 26, he makes two points that might help youth understand what's going on in this story.

First, when Jesus says, "You always have the poor with you, but you won't always have me," it's hard not to think Jesus is being a bit of a jerk. Doesn't that go against what he's been teaching? Not quite. In his commentary, Wesley writes that God is actually telling us that we will have the opportunity to help relieve the wants of others. The opportunity to help others is a gift.

Second, even though Jesus' death is coming soon, it appears clear that the woman had no intention of anointing Jesus for his burial. She did what she felt led to do. This shows the hand of God at work in preparing the disciples for the coming death of Jesus.

Foot-Washing: John 13:1-20

In his writing, Wesley addresses Peter's statement where he refuses to let Jesus wash him. Jesus' response of "Unless I wash you, you won't have a place with me" shows the significance of the cleansing his death will bring to humanity. His sacrifice is what "washed" Peter. This was, like baptism, an outward sign of an inward change. Jesus says Peter won't have a place with him unless Peter is washed. This is particularly strong language, especially when you are reading through the prism of presence and community with one another.

The Last Supper: Mark 14:10-26 and 1 Corinthians 11:23-26

In his writing about 1 Corinthians 11:24, which reads, "This is my body, which is for you; do this to remember me," Wesley draws special attention to the attitude we bring when come to the Communion Table. It is yet another time when we are present together as a community of children of God, and Wesley reminds us that we should take part in this ceremony in a humble, thankful, and obedient way. It is a time of community and presence with one another as we remember the suffering that Jesus endured on our behalf.

Leader Reflection

In John 15, Jesus introduces us to a life-changing discovery. He says that his followers will no longer be identified by their adherence to rules and laws, but instead they will be known by their love. In verses 9-12, Jesus can't stop talking about the importance of love.

He wants us all to love one another as he has loved us. Love is revealed in the way we serve and care for another. It's revealed when we think of the needs of others before our own.

Yet, in today's culture, it's hard to remember how to be known by our love. How do we show our love with our lifestyle? How do we show our love as youth leaders? Would our students identify us by our love?

I am guilty of getting caught up in my own agenda for my youth, planning activities and events while failing to pay attention to what the youth actually need. However, my most powerful and empowering moments in ministry have been those quiet moments where I simply sit with a student and let that student talk, where I show my love by merely being present.

As you embark on this lesson with your students, keep in mind that the underlying message in all you say and do is love. They'll remember that far more than anything you actually say.

Love and be loved.

NOTES

SYNC (10-15 minutes)

High-Energy Option—Better Together

SAY: Today we're going to do something really cool, but it requires depending on one another. First, I'm going to need everyone to get into groups of five. Each group is going to need four chairs. This activity requires some steps, so listen carefully. You are going to create a human table.

[Allow groups time to get together and to collect the chairs they'll need.]

SAY: Now, working together, we're going to walk through the following steps from your Student Journal.

STEP 1: Position your chairs in a tight circle, facing inward.

STEP 2: Have four of your group members sit down in the chairs sideways with their feet touching the ground. Make sure everyone is facing counterclockwise.

STEP 3: One at a time, lie backward, resting your head on the legs of the person behind you.

STEP 4: Once everyone is lying backward, the fifth person should VERY carefully remove the chairs from under each person one at a time. You may need to adjust so you're resting your full weight on your legs and the lap of the person behind you.

SAY: Hold this position for just a few moments. Then the fifth person will put the chairs back under your group members as quickly as possible so you can sit back up.

ASK: When I told you you'd be forming a human table, did you believe it would happen? What was it like when the chair was taken out from under you?

[Allow for responses.]

SAY: Our lesson today is about the importance of being together. This activity shows us that we can do more together than we can alone.

Low-Energy Option—Drawing in the Dark

[Before class, choose two or three objects that will be difficult to describe. You will need one object for each pair of volunteers you choose for the activity.]

SAY: For this activity, I'll need six volunteers *(two volunteers for each object)*. You'll need to pair up with one of the other volunteers. One of you will be blindfolded and asked to draw something, and the other will be describing the item for you to draw. You cannot say what the item is; you can only describe it. Choose who wants to describe and who wants to draw.

[Let the students pick their tasks and have the first team step to a flip chart at the front of the room. Blindfold the drawing student before giving the describer an object.]

SAY: You will have 30 seconds to describe the object to your partner, and then they will have 45 seconds to draw what they think the object looks like while still blindfolded. Go!

[Repeat this process with each of the pairs. Be sure to save each drawing so that you can compare them later.]

SAY: Okay, I need each of our drawers at the chart again. I'm going to give you 30 seconds to hold the item you drew, and then 30 seconds to draw it again. Ready? Go!

[Allow drawers an opportunity to draw another drawing beside or underneath their previous drawing.]

SAY: Okay, take off the blindfolds! How do you think you did?

ASK: Which drawings look the closest to the object they were given? Which process led to more accurate drawings?

SAY: Sometimes the best way to help someone understand something is to let them experience it for themselves. Our lesson today explores that further.

TOUR (20-25 minutes)

[In this section, students will move from station to station tracing out the narrative of Jesus from the anointing until the Last Supper in order to trace the themes found throughout. Before the class begins, set up the stations as follows.]

Station One: essential oil

Station Two: a towel, a washcloth, and a bowl of water

Station Three: a loaf of bread and a cup of grape juice

Station Four: an empty table

SAY: We're going to explore four Scriptures that all discuss the importance of community and lead up to and describe the Last Supper with Jesus and his disciples. We'll read each passage at a different station and participate in a small act to help you remember what you've heard. After each station, take a moment to record your experiences in your Student Journal.

[Move to Station One.]

SAY: I need a volunteer to read Matthew 26:6-13. As the passage is read, I want each of you to take a drop of the essential oil and place it on your wrist to remember the way Jesus was anointed.

[Have the volunteer read the passage as students place the essential oil on their wrists. Allow them a moment or two after the reading to write down their reflections. Move to Station Two.]

SAY: I'll need another volunteer to read John 13:1-20. As the volunteer reads this passage about Jesus washing the disciples' feet, I want you to dip the washcloth in the bowl of water and let the water run over your hand. Think about what Jesus and his disciples would have been experiencing during this time.

[Let the volunteer read John 13:1-20 as the students dip the washcloth into the water and wring it out. Give them a moment or two to write down their reflections. Move to Station Three.]

SAY: I'll need a volunteer to read Mark 14:10-26. While this person reads about the Last Supper, break off a piece of bread and dip it into the cup. As you eat the bread, consider the emotions of Jesus and his disciples during the Last Supper.

[The volunteer will read Mark 14:10-26 as the students eat the bread and dip it into the cup. Allow the students time to write down their reflections in their Student Journals. Move to Station Four.]

SAY: As I read the final passage, focus on the empty table and consider the other Scriptures we've read tonight. Think about the importance of Jesus' presence in these moments and how we can continue to remember Jesus and be present with one another.

[Read 1 Corinthians 11:23-26. Pause for a moment after the verse is complete, then allow the students to write their reflections in their journals.]

ASK: Did you learn more from the words in these passages or from the actions Jesus did within them? Why?

[Allow for a few answers.]

ASK: What surprised you about this experience tonight?

[Allow for one or two responses.]

SAY: Before we finish this part of the lesson, we're going to watch a video that puts into action much of what we've experienced tonight.

[Show "Pope celebrates Holy Thursday"—four minutes https://www.youtube.com/watch?v=zXS5j9Q1Wrg.]

SAY: Early in 2016, the Pope changed a rule and began allowing women to participate in the foot-washing ceremony at the Vatican. He also washed the feet of Syrian refugees, Muslims, Orthodox Christians, and Hindus, in addition to Catholics.

ASK: What can we learn from this video? What does this video mean to you in light of what you've experienced today?

[Allow for as many responses as possible.]

SAY: In the passages we read today, Jesus showed us compassion and humility. He welcomed the woman who anointed his feet, washed his disciples' feet even though he was their leader, and shared his final meal with them, even with the one who would betray him. When others would have scoffed or scorned others, Jesus broke the barriers of what was socially acceptable to invite others into community.

REVEAL (10 minutes)

SAY: For the next few minutes, I want you to imagine the following scenarios and journal about how they would make you feel.

SCENARIO ONE: Youth group is about to start, and everyone is sitting in a circle waiting for your youth leader to begin the lesson. All of a sudden, a strange woman enters the room and wordlessly begins to pour essential oil on the feet of your youth leader and washes them with a towel. As this happens, your youth leader continues with the lesson completely unfazed. What would you say? Would it make you uncomfortable? Why?

[After three or four minutes, direct the students to the second scenario.]

SCENARIO TWO: It's Christmas dinner, and you're gathered together with your best friends and closest family. As the meal is about to begin, the host begins to talk about his or her coming death and asks you to think of him or her each time you gather together to eat this specific meal in the future. How would you respond? Would it make you uncomfortable? Why?

[Allow a few minutes for responses.]

SAY: If you feel comfortable, I'd like to invite a few of you to share your responses with the class.

ASK: How did it affect your view of these stories to see them recast in this light?

BUILD (15 minutes)

SAY: Using your experiences and reflections from this lesson, I want you to create your own scene about what you think the Last Supper was like. Be creative and try to depict it differently than the ways you've seen it before. You can paint a picture or write a song. Maybe you want to set it in the future or maybe show it from the perspective of one of the disciples. Whatever you choose, make sure it showcases something you feel is important about this event.

[Make paint, markers, and paper available to students, as well as pens and pencils. If you have a student who is musically inclined, you may even want a guitar available. Allow the students ten minutes to create their versions of the Last Supper.]

ASK: Who wants to share your version of the Last Supper? What's unique about your depiction? Why did you choose to highlight that?

AFTER (5 minutes)

[Invite the students to participate in one of the After activities this week. Send them a reminder during the week about what they choose.]

Different Dinner Tables

SAY: This week take some time at lunch to ask your friends what a regular weeknight dinner looks like at their house. What do they eat? Who is there? Do they enjoy it or do they wish it were different? Think about their experience in relation to what goes on at your home.

Being Present

SAY: Nursing-home residents and people who are homebound can feel very lonely, especially if they no longer have family. Ask your leader or the church office for a list of names and addresses of church members who live in nursing homes or can no longer get out of their homes. Write letters or send cards to them. Invite your recipients to write back to you. You might even make a new friend!

#PassionPresence

SAY: Take a picture with your family or group of friends and share it on social media along with your feelings about what it means to be present with them in tough times. Use *#PassionPresence* to tag your picture.

PRAYER

SAY: We're going to close this class in prayer. Silently say the prayer in your Student Journals along with me.

[Silently pray:]

God, just like Jesus came to be present with us, help me be present with others. Especially with

---

[Pray the following out loud:]

ALL: Therefore, let's draw near to God with a genuine heart, with the certainty that our faith gives us, since our hearts are sprinkled clean and our bodies are washed pure with water. Amen.

Betrayal

Summary

In this lesson, students will explore disappointment and betrayal from those they love and make steps toward forgiveness and peace.

Overview

- **Sync** students with the disappointment and frustration that happens when people don't do what they should through a group activity.
- **Tour** through Matthew 26 to explore the concepts of friendship, peace, and forgiveness, in spite of betrayal and disappointment.
- **Reveal** to each other scenarios where forgiveness is needed and advise each other on how to proceed in light of Jesus' example.
- **Build** a "peace treaty" for an area of conflict in the life of your students to help them find tangible ways to pursue peace.
- **After** the lesson, challenge the students to show forgiveness this week to themselves and to others.

Anchor Point

- Matthew 26:50—*But Jesus said to him, "Friend, do what you came to do."*

Supplies

- Student Journals
- Pens or pencils
- Sheets of paper
- Projectable image of Giotto's painting *The Arrest of Christ*

Parent E-mail

This week we are talking about betrayal and being disappointed by people we love. Youth will be challenged to face difficult situations and create a pathway to forgiveness and peace. Here are some things you can do this week to help your student:

- Around the dinner table, share something that has been troubling you at work and ask your kids what they think you should do. Then ask if they'll pray for you.
- Invite them to share a difficult situation with you, and promise to pray for them concerning each child's specific scenario. The key here is to listen.

Leader Notes

Rejection evokes a lot of strong emotions. These emotions can be even stronger in teenagers when the struggles of adolescence are overwhelmingly raw. As this lesson progresses, take special note of any emotional responses from your youth. This might allow the opening for one-on-one conversations in the coming week. As in the previous two lessons, the key is to be present with your youth. It's not about what you say; it's about creating a safe and open space. Don't force conversation, but open the floor for it.

If you have a personal story connected with betrayal and forgiveness, consider sharing it with your students. If you aren't sure if it's appropriate, ask one of your helpers or your pastor what they think. Vulnerability goes two ways, but only if it's shared in a healthy way.

Theology and Commentary

The Garden

Jesus' time with the disciples in the garden of Gethsemane contrasts the humanity of Jesus with the humanity of the disciples. We are shown a version of Jesus who is in despair. He cries out to God to take this burden from him, but ultimately he knows that he must do God's will. This is what humanity is capable of—even in pain and fear, we can do what God calls us to do.

The disciples, on the other hand, show us the frailty of humanity. They are confused and tired. It has already been a difficult evening emotionally, and they cannot stay awake. Jesus is disappointed, but continues on in spite of their weakness.

The Arrest

Three of the four Gospels point to the kiss Judas gave Jesus as a pivotal part in the Passion narrative. A man kissing another man in this era would have symbolized great respect and honor. By identifying Jesus through this action, as an act of betrayal, Judas was communicating an extreme amount of disrespect. We can see it as a sign of even deeper betrayal by viewing it through this lens.

In Matthew 27, we read of Judas's attempt to undo what he's done. This speaks to our innate impulse to try and undo the wrongs we've done. In his overwhelming guilt, Judas kills himself. Despite the loving forgiveness Jesus exuded toward all he encountered, it was Judas's judgment of himself that led to his demise.

Many have hypothesized that Judas did not betray Jesus out of malice, but instead did so because he believed Jesus would be an earthly king. By turning Jesus over to the authorities, he may have intended to spark a revolution in which Jesus and his followers overthrew the Roman government and the religious leadership in Jerusalem. However, if this was Judas's intention, it is clear that he misunderstood the fundamental nature of Jesus' mission.

The Trial

Matthew's depiction of Jesus' trial in front of the high priests, legal experts, and elders casts these traditional religious figures in a very poor light. In an attempt to maintain their power and prestige, they are shown neglecting the very laws they say they are trying to protect. They even allow people to bear false witness against Jesus during this trial, something that the Ten Commandments, and therefore Jewish law, very clearly oppose.

Additionally, when Jesus refuses to respond in the way they desire, they spit on him, disgrace him, and abuse him. These religious leaders show themselves for who they truly are in their interaction with Jesus.

The Denial

When reading Peter's denial, we often recall Jesus' prediction in Luke 22 that Peter would deny him. However, even that doesn't explain the depth of Peter's denial. Peter denies Jesus to a servant girl and other people of low social status who likely could not have harmed him. He is that scared to admit that he knows Jesus. He also makes a pledge that he doesn't know Jesus. This is exactly the kind of oath Jesus spoke against in Matthew 5. In denying Jesus, Peter is simultaneously violating Jesus' teachings.

Peter's denial in Matthew 26 can also be contrasted with Judas's response to his own act of betrayal found in Matthew 27. Both of them betray Jesus, but while Peter eventually finds forgiveness after Jesus' resurrection, Judas falls into despair and kills himself.

Leader Reflection

I pray you are feeling nourished and loved this week. If you aren't, please take a few moments right now and do something you love. Listen to your favorite song; go for a short walk or run; or just grab a latte, take a seat, and enjoy it.

In this lesson, you will be teaching your kids about disappointment, forgiveness, and seeking peace. Before you teach this week, I urge you to make peace with yourself. Our youth rarely know what baggage we carry when we aren't with them, but we carry it nonetheless. Give yourself the space to feel at peace with who you are. Forgive yourself for the ways you think you don't measure up, and ask for God's forgiveness and love to spring up within you.

Take some time this week and read this verse silently:

2 Timothy 1:7—"God didn't give us a spirit that is timid but one that is powerful, loving, and self-controlled."

Write it out below. Take time to consider each word as you write it.

_____

_____

_____

Now read it aloud.

Embrace the spirit that God gave you: one that is powerful, loving, and self-controlled.

NOTES

_____

_____

_____

SYNC (5-10 minutes)

High-Energy Option—Stand Up!

[Before class, pull a few students aside and instruct them not to help their partners stand up during the first part of the activity. Choose a few others and instruct them not to stand up during the second part of the activity.]

SAY: Everyone, find a partner! Once you have your partner, sit down on the floor back-to-back. Link arms with your partner and, together, try to stand up without using your hands.

[Give the students a few moments to try. Hopefully, a few teams will be successful, while others will be thwarted by the students you planted.]

SAY: Now let's try that same activity with a larger group. I need three volunteers.

[Let the group of three try and stand. Keep adding students to the group, making sure to include the students you've planted for the second activity.]

ASK: Some of you seemed to have a hard time with this activity. What made it so frustrating? Why?

[Give the students an opportunity to answer. Allow the disruptive students to reveal that they were working against their partners on purpose.]

SAY: It can be really exciting when we work together to do something, but it can also be disheartening when one person gives up or works against the group. Today we're going to explore this disappointment.

Low-Energy Option—Storytelling

SAY: Go ahead and get in groups of five. Each person is going to need one piece of paper and a pen. I need one person per group to come up here to get the paper and pens.

[When the students come up to get the supplies, instruct them to do the opposite of what you tell everyone else to do in this activity. Their goal is to disrupt the process without anyone noticing.]

SAY: You will have thirty seconds to write a one-sentence story at the top of your paper. Once you've written your sentence, fold the paper over just enough to cover what you wrote. Try to only use the top inch or so of the paper.

[Give the students thirty seconds to write their sentences.]

SAY: Now, pass the paper to the person on your right. They will read your sentence and draw a picture to explain what you wrote. Fold the paper again to cover the drawing.

[Give the students thirty to forty-five seconds to make their drawings.]

SAY: Pass the papers to the right again. This time, write a sentence about the picture you see. Keep trading back-and-forth until you get your original paper back.

[Give the students a few minutes to do the next few rounds. When they receive their original sheet, there should be a lot of confusion.]

ASK: Did things turn out like you expected? Were there any surprises? What do you think happened?

[Give the students a few minutes to share, and allow the disrupting students to reveal the secret instructions you gave them.]

SAY: It's fun to build something together, but it can be disappointing when one person intentionally throws everything off.

TOUR (20 minutes)

ASK: Raise your hands—who here has ever made a mistake?

[Everyone raises their hands.]

ASK: What did you do when you got caught? Did you try to deny it?

[Allow for two or three responses.]

SAY: Today we're going to read about the night of Jesus' arrest, especially the role of Peter and of Jesus' disciples. I'll need three volunteers to read from the Book of Matthew.

[Assign one of the following passages to each volunteer: Matthew 26:36-46; Matthew 26:47-56; Matthew 26:57-68.]

SAY: All right. As we listen to our first reading, I want everyone to kneel. Consider what is going through the disciples' minds throughout this passage.

[Have the first volunteer read Matthew 26:36-46.]

ASK: When Jesus was in the garden praying, why do you think he wanted his disciples to stay awake and pray with him?

[Allow for a brief discussion. Invite the students to come up with a variety of reasons.]

SAY: We're going to listen to our second reading of the night. As we listen, I want you to focus on the picture at the front of the room and think about what from this passage you see in this painting.

[On a projector or TV screen, put up an image of the painting The Arrest of Christ by Giotto di Bondone. It can be found on Wikiart.org. Have the second volunteer read Matthew 26:47-56.]

ASK: What parts of the Scripture do you see in this painting of the event? Is this how you've pictured Jesus' betrayal? What did you think would be different?

[Allow for a brief discussion. Invite the students to re-read the passage in their Student Journals to search out different parts of the Scripture that are included in the painting.]

SAY: For our third reading tonight, I want you to underline all the responses and actions of Jesus. Consider what was going through Jesus' mind as this was all happening.

[Have the third volunteer read Matthew 26:57-68.]

ASK: How did Jesus act in the face of these accusations? What did he say? Why do you think he responded this way?

[Allow for a brief discussion. Have the students consider how they would have responded similarly or differently.]

SAY: For our final reading, I'm going to need a few more volunteers to read the story and act it out.

[Choose youth to be the narrator, Peter, the servant woman, and the woman by the gate. The whole class will read the crowd's line (All) from verse 73. Have the narrator start the reading, with the rest of the class reading their parts.]

ASK: It's easy to judge Peter here for denying that he knew Jesus, but have you ever denied something when you found yourself in an uncomfortable situation?

[Allow for a few students to share times when they denied doing something that they had done.]

SAY: His friends fell asleep while he was trying to pray. One of his followers sold him out for a bag of money. He was accused of disrespecting God by the very people who should have known to worship him. And one of his closest friends denied even knowing him. Consider the feeling of betrayal and disappointment that Jesus must have felt.

SAY: Jesus knew he was going to be disregarded by some of the people he loved most, yet he still loved them and spent time with them.

ASK: Are you surprised by the way Jesus responded? Do you think you'd be able to respond in the same way?

[Allow for a brief discussion.]

ASK: What are we supposed to do when those close to us let us down and disappoint us?

[Allow for a few responses.]

SAY: In Matthew 26:50, Jesus says to Judas, "Friend, do what you came to do." Let that sink sin. Jesus still called Judas *friend* and still ate with Judas hours before, even knowing Judas was about to betray him.

ASK: Do you think Jesus would have forgiven Judas if Judas had asked for it? Why or why not?

[Allow for a longer discussion. Invite the students to disagree with one another; this is a difficult question.]

REVEAL (10 minutes)

SAY: For this activity, you're going to need a partner. You're going to be sharing with this person, so it's best if you partner up with someone you trust to give you good feedback.

[Allow the students a moment to pair up.]

SAY: Spend the next few minutes and write out a scenario from the recent past where someone hurt you or you hurt someone else. Focus on emotions and the way each of you has responded. The specifics aren't as important as the broad strokes of the experience.

[Give the students three minutes to write out their scenarios.]

SAY: Trade Student Journals with your partner. Read what your partner wrote and then respond with advice for them based on the example of Jesus from our lesson today. How can we apply that thinking toward making peace in this situation?

[Give the students three minutes to respond.]

SAY: Give your partners their Student Journals back so they can read what you wrote for them. Would anyone like to share your scenario and the advice you received?

[Allow two or three students to share.]

BUILD (10 minutes)

SAY: God has often been used as an excuse for people to hold on to anger and resentment. Throughout history, a lot of wars have been blamed on God. However, when Jesus was betrayed, he did not fight back. He showed mercy and forgiveness. What does that mean for us?

[Allow for a few answers. Affirm all responses.]

ASK: Who knows what a peace treaty is? How does it work? *(Answer: Both sides give up something and agree to live in peace with each other.)*

SAY: Today you're going to create a peace treaty in your Student Journal. This can be a peace treaty between two friends, family members, groups of people, or even countries, if you so choose. Remember, peace works both ways. Both sides have to give on something. There has to be one person to extend the peace offering, and the other has to accept it so they can live in peace together.

[Allow the students five minutes to write their treaties.]

SAY: If you feel comfortable, come up to the front and share your treaty.

AFTER (5 minutes)

[Invite the students to participate in an After activity. Send them a reminder during the week.]

Peace With Others

SAY: Think of someone you have often had a contentious relationship with—maybe it's a parent or a teacher or a classmate. This week do a kind act for this person or send a note saying why you appreciate her or him. Don't look for attention; just do it because it's a good thing to do.

Peace With Yourself

SAY: This week sit down for fifteen or twenty minutes and write yourself a letter of forgiveness. In the future, whenever you start to feel angry at yourself for one reason or another, pull out your letter and remind yourself of this forgiveness.

Peace From God

SAY: This week look for signs of God's forgiveness and mercy in the world around you. When you find one, take a picture and post it on social media. Use *#PassionPeace* to highlight what you've found.

PRAYER

SAY: Let's all pray together.

God,

We all know how hard it is to forgive someone for hurting us. And we all know how it feels to hurt someone else. Help us remember what both of those things feel like when we are faced with difficult situations. May we always act in the way that shows your love.

Amen.

Alone

Summary

Students will explore the topics of pain and abandonment. They will also explore how to respond with love to those who suffer.

Overview

- **Sync** students with the concept that we are stronger when we work together instead of isolating ourselves.
- **Tour** through the story of Jesus' trial and execution to understand how Jesus dealt with suffering.
- **Reveal** how the students relate to the suffering and vulnerability of Jesus by having them reflect on their own experiences of suffering.
- **Build** a clay representation of how the students can serve those who are suffering or alone.
- **After** the lesson, the students will be challenged to consider the needs of others and think about how they can show love for others this week.

Anchor Point

- Luke 23:34—*Jesus said, "Father, forgive them, for they don't know what they're doing."*

Supplies

- Student Journals
- Pens or pencils
- Socks, food items, or other items to be donated to charity
- Hula-Hoops
- Blindfold
- Peanut butter, jelly, bread, knife, plate
- Clay
- Quiet background music

Parent E-mail

This is the last week of our Passion study. This week your student will reflect on times when she or he has felt abandoned and/or alone. Here are some ways to engage this week:

- Spend time brainstorming something your family can do to help those who are suffering in some capacity. Make this a priority.
- This week write your student a letter describing the good traits you see in him or her. Often, students can feel isolated from their parents, and by taking time to tangibly and specifically encourage your kids, they will be reminded of the support they have in you.

Leader Notes

When faced with rejection, abandonment, and loneliness, many teens respond with bitterness. As conversations flow throughout this lesson, make an effort to challenge youth to respond in a more positive way.

Our experiences of suffering and isolation can also leave us feeling lost. Help your youth discover ways that these struggles can be turned around to help us find a new purpose.

Theology and Commentary

When you're studying the crucifixion of Jesus, it's inevitable that there will be some conversation about salvation and atonement. There are a number of different atonement theologies prevalent in Christian theology, and it'll be useful for you to have a basic understanding of them in case they come up.

Simply put, atonement theologies are ways to discuss the way God finds reconciliation with humanity and saves us through Christ. Some pithier scholars refer to it as "at-one-ment," meaning that we are meant to be one with God. The process of atonement bridges the gap.

Moral Influence Theory

Moral influence theory suggests that the purpose of Christianity is to make us morally good. In this theory, Jesus came to earth to give humans a good moral example. In this case, the purpose of Jesus is not in his death, but rather in his life. Atonement is achieved when we live like Jesus taught us.

Ransom Theory

This theory presents humanity as enslaved to sin and death, and thus in need of rescue. It essentially pits Jesus against Satan. The life of Jesus serves as the "ransom" for our souls so that we might have eternal life.

Satisfaction Theory

In this understanding, instead of humanity needing to be rescued from Satan, humans owe a debt to God. The "insult" of sin is considered too great to simply be forgiven, and the ultimate sacrifice (Jesus) is the only way humanity can satisfy this debt. Christ's death is considered to be not a way of defeating Satan, but rather a way of fulfilling our debt to God.

Penal Substitution Theory

This theory is related to the satisfaction theory. In penal substitution, the emphasis moves away from paying a debt and toward humanity deserving punishment for our sins. Had Jesus not died for our sins, we would have to face eternal death. When we break God's law, that is sin and these sins bring on the punishment of God. In this theory, Jesus takes our punishments so that we don't have to.

Your theological beliefs may match up fully with one of these theories, or none of them. You may view atonement as a combination of multiple theories. Scot McKnight refers to atonement theologies as golf clubs: each is appropriate in the right situation, but none are right all the time.[1] No matter where you come down, it's important to know some of the common ways people think about atonement and Jesus' death and resurrection. This will help you listen and guide your students as they wrestle with this story.

The purpose of this is not to evoke guilt and shame because of our sins. It's also not about deciding which theology is right and which is wrong. Both of those approaches make the Passion too much about us. The goal in this lesson is to take what we can learn, based in our own understandings, and use it to change the way we live and love.

1. See Scot McKnight, *A Community Called Atonement* (Nashville: Abingdon Press, 2007).

Leader Reflection

My time in youth ministry has been full of mountains and valleys. I'm sure you've experienced the same. One year, in particular, was really tough. The church where I worked endured a never-ending stream of problems. Simultaneously, I was battling depression and anxiety. I was done. I felt drained, overworked, afraid that I'd been abandoned by God.

That year I attended a Maundy Thursday service where a friend read Psalm 22. As he was reading, the lights were turned off one at a time, and darkness spread over the sanctuary. I vividly remember sitting there, feeling like God had left and that I was alone.

It was the first time I'd every truly related to that vulnerable pain found in this psalm. The words felt like they were already residing within me. On the drive home, I looked out the window as the landscape unfolded in the dark, and it seemed as if even nature felt lost and forsaken.

I share all this with you because I want you to know you aren't alone. I want to encourage you to be strengthened by your struggles. Ministry is challenging, but it isn't meant to defeat you. This lesson looks at feelings of abandonment and loneliness. So many in ministry struggle with these feelings.

This week read Psalm 22 and let it speak to you. Be aware of the ways you feel abandoned, and let them make you stronger as you continue on in your good work.

NOTES

SYNC (5-10 minutes)

High-Energy Option—Hula Roundup

[Before class, gather several pairs of socks, food items, and anything else that can be donated to charity. Make sure there's at least one item per student.]

SAY: This game requires three teams.

[Let students separate themselves into teams.]

SAY: Each team will be given a Hula-Hoop. Your goal is to get all of the items inside of your hoop. The game is over when all of the items are in one hoop. You can get items at any time, and you can even take them out of other teams' hoops. Ready? Go!

[It should be impossible to do this with everyone taking from one another. They may figure this out quickly or it could take awhile. After a few moments, suggest to one of the teams that they could put all three hoops together and then everyone would win.]

ASK: Did you find that frustrating? Why was it so difficult?

[Wait for a few responses.]

ASK: What do you think the point of this activity was? *(When we act selflessly, everyone wins.)*

SAY: Today we're going to explore what it feels like to be alone and what we can do as a community to work together and support one another.

Low-Energy Option—Make Me a Sandwich

SAY: I need a volunteer who knows their way around a kitchen and doesn't have a nut allergy.

[Blindfold the volunteer and have them sit at a table. In front of them, place the necessary supplies for a peanut-butter-and-jelly sandwich.]

SAY (to the volunteer): In front of you, I've placed everything you'll need to make a peanut-butter-and-jelly sandwich. You have ninety seconds to make it. Go!

SAY (to the rest of the class): Don't give any hints. Let's see what happens.

[Start a timer and stop the volunteer after ninety seconds.]

SAY (to the volunteer): How do you think you did? Want to try again? This time we'll give you help.

SAY (to the rest of the class): All right. This time you can give all the hints you want. Make sure they're helpful! Go!

[Set the timer and stop the volunteer after ninety seconds. Have the volunteer take off the blindfold.]

ASK: Which attempt worked the best? Why did it work better? Was it hard to watch your friend try to make a sandwich blindfolded without being able to help?

[Allow for as many responses as possible.]

SAY: Today we're going to explore what it feels like to be alone and what we can do as a community to make sure we support one another in tough times.

TOUR (15-20 minutes)

SAY: This is our final study on the Passion of Jesus. Using what we've learned in the past three weeks as well as what we'll be reading about today, I want to home in on what makes Jesus' love for us so powerful and why he would endure so much as a result.

We're going to break our time tonight into three parts. First, we're going to talk about Pontius Pilate. This is one of those scenarios where you know that the people involved had no idea how much impact their choices would have. As we read the following passage, consider how you would have handled this situation if you had been in Pilate's place. I'll need a volunteer to read aloud.

[Have your student volunteer read Matthew 27:17-24.]

ASK: Have you ever been in a situation where you didn't act and wished later that you had? What changed?

[Allow for three or four responses. Ask the students how they feel their situations are similar to the story of Pilate.]

ASK: Have you ever seen something and thought, *Well, that's not my problem*? Maybe someone was getting picked on and you walked past, choosing to stay out of it.

[If the conversation is going well, bring up the following point. Otherwise, move on to the section about Luke 23:32-43.]

SAY: Desmond Tutu, a South-African bishop and civil rights leader, once said:

> If you are neutral in situations of injustice, you have chosen the side of the oppressor. If an elephant has its foot on the tail of a mouse and you say that you are neutral, the mouse will not appreciate your neutrality.

ASK: What does that mean to you? Do you think Pilate considered the ramifications his choice would have for Jesus and the world?

[Give a few students the opportunity to respond.]

SAY: Okay, let's move on and look at Jesus on his way to the cross. I need a volunteer to read Luke 23:32-43. As our volunteer reads this passage, circle the verse that sticks out to you the most.

[Have a student volunteer read Luke 23:32-43.]

ASK: What stuck out to you the most from this passage of Scripture?

[Give three or four students the opportunity to respond. When they tell you what struck them, keep responding, "Why?" to dig deeper into why it impacted them.]

ASK: Have you ever been in a situation where you felt the need to prove yourself, but you knew that would make things worse?

[Allow a few responses.]

ASK: When is it hard for you to show mercy?

[Allow a few responses.]

SAY: For our last section today, I'm going to need a volunteer to read Mark 15:33-39.

[Have a student volunteer read Mark 15:33-39.]

SAY: In this passage we get to see Jesus' strength and his vulnerability. Jesus wasn't ashamed to cry out to God. He wasn't ashamed to question God. Jesus knows, better than anyone, the strength and power in sharing our heart's cry with others, even if they can't understand.

ASK: What do you think when you see people share their deepest emotions? Does it make you uncomfortable? Why or why not?

[Allow everyone who wants to respond to answer.]

SAY: Think back on everything we've learned over the past few weeks. Looking back on the humility Jesus showed as he entered Jerusalem, the way he washed the disciples' feet, even the way he responded to his accusers, we can see a whole new way of life being laid out for us. We can connect with the raw pain and betrayal Jesus felt the last two days of his life. In the most horrific week of his life, Jesus taught us how to be truly, deeply human.

ASK: What sticks out to you most from what we've studied about the Passion over the last four weeks?

[Go around the room and allow each student to answer. Ask each of them to explain their answer a bit more.]

REVEAL (10 minutes)

SAY: This study is called the Passion. Contrary to the way we might use that word, this term comes from the Greek word *pascho* and means "to experience suffering." Over the last few weeks, we've been learning about the experiences of Jesus leading up to his crucifixion and death. We've been learning about his experience of suffering on our behalf.

I want you to take a few moments and journal about what it has meant to you to reflect on Jesus' experience. Ask yourself what it has felt like when you've gone through suffering. What did it feel like when you seemed to be alone or abandoned?

Take a few minutes now to reflect on those questions.

[Give the students five minutes to respond.]

SAY: If you feel comfortable, share what you wrote with someone else in the class. Read what they wrote as well. In their journal, write a prayer for them that will help them remember the Passion.

[Give the students three minutes to write their prayers.]

SAY: All right. Hand back the Student Journal to the person you traded with. Spend a moment and silently pray the prayer your partner wrote for you.

BUILD (15 minutes)

SAY: When discussing this part of Jesus' story, it's only natural to talk about the intense feeling of loneliness he must have experienced. You probably feel this intense loneliness at times as well. You might feel lost in your busy schedule or you might feel like you aren't seen. But I want you to know that you are. You are seen, and you are loved.

Today each of you is going to be given a piece of clay. Spend the next few minutes thinking about the things in the world that cause so much suffering that you can't ignore them. Think about the things you want to help change.

[Pause for a minute or two to allow the students time to reflect.]

SAY: Now, take the piece of clay and shape it into something that represents what you feel called to change. As happened with Jesus, our greatest pain can sometimes produce our greatest acts of love.

[Pass out clay and allow the students seven or eight minutes to fashion their clay. Play some light music to help the students focus.]

SAY: One at a time, bring your clay to the front, share what you've made, and add it to our larger piece of clay.

[Have an older student or adult volunteer shape the separate pieces of clay into a large cross. You may want to have a hymn playing in the background as the students do this.]

SAY: Jesus came to show us a new way of life. He came to be the change the world needs. When we live like Jesus, we will experience both joy and pain. But if we find genuine love at the root of all we do, the struggle is worth it.

AFTER (5 minutes)

[Invite the students to participate in an After activity. Send them a reminder during the week.]

Feel Their Feelings

SAY: This week when you feel hurt or upset, pause and think of someone else who might be feeling a similar way. Send a text or leave a note to encourage that person.

Homemade Sacrifice

SAY: Jesus was aware of the needs of those around him. In fact, he sacrificed to meet so many of their needs. This week think of something you can sacrifice at home to make life easier for someone in your family.

Not Alone

SAY: A lot of people use social media so that they will feel more connected to their friends and not feel lonely. This week go out of your way to comment on the social media posts of a friend or classmate you don't typically interact with to assure this person that you are thinking of him or her and they are not alone.

PRAYER

SAY: Let's all pray the following words from Isaiah together.

But now, LORD, you are our father.
We are the clay, and you are our potter.
All of us are the work of your hand. — Isaiah 64:8

Lord, shape us so we may bring your loving passion to this world.

Amen.

Explore More

The Crucifixion

Anchor Point
• Mark 15:22-29

Summary

Jesus endures overwhelming suffering and mockery while he is on the cross. While on the cross, Jesus cries out to God and eventually dies. The events of his death lead those nearby to realize who he was.

Takeaways

• During his crucifixion, those nearby continue to hurl insults at Jesus, but upon his death and the events connected to it, they begin to realize that he was who he said he was.

Why Did Jesus Have to Die?

Anchor Point
• John 3:1-21

Summary

In this passage, Jesus meets with Nicodemus, a well-educated Pharisee. Nicodemus approaches Jesus in the dark of night, to see if Jesus is who he says he is. This conversation serves as a good summary of who Jesus is and why he came.

Takeaways

• Jesus explains that he was sent not to judge the world, but to save the world.
• Nicodemus approaches Jesus at night and Jesus ends this conversation with a series of statements about light and darkness, and how the light exposes the truth.

FATH⬤M

A deeper dive into understanding the key themes and storylines of the Bible

Continue Your Journey Into God's Story With The Following Fathom Titles

To learn more about all 18 Studies go to
YouthMinistryPartners.com/Studies/Fathom

Printed in the USA
CPSIA information can be obtained
at www.ICGtesting.com
LVHW03075720l123
764199LV00010B/150